WITHDRAWN

Easy Crafts in **5** steps

Easy Earth-Friendly Crafts in 5 Steps

Enslow Elementary

an imprint of

 Enslow Publishers, Inc.

40 Industrial Road
Box 398
Berkeley Heights, NJ 07922
USA

http://www.enslow.com

PORTER MEMORIAL BRANCH LIBRARY
NEWTON COUNTY LIBRARY SYSTEM
6191 HIGHWAY 212
COVINGTON, GA 30016

Note to Kids: The materials used in this book are suggestions. If you do not have an item, use something similar. Use any color material and paint that you wish. Use your imagination!

Safety Note: Be sure to ask for help from an adult, if needed, to complete these crafts.

Note to Teachers and Parents: Crafts are prepared using air-drying clay. Please follow package directions. Children may use color clay or they may paint using poster paint once clay is completely dry. The colors used is this book are suggestions. Children may use any color clay, cardboard, pencils, or paint they wish. Let them use their imaginations!

Enslow Elementary, an imprint of Enslow Publishers, Inc.
Enslow Elementary® is a registered trademark of Enslow Publishers, Inc.

English edition copyright © 2008 by Enslow Publishers, Inc.

All rights reserved.

No part of this book may be reproduced by any means without the written permission of the publisher.

Translated from the Spanish edition by Ian Grenzeback, edited by Jaime Ramírez-Castilla, of Strictly Spanish, LLC. Edited and produced by Enslow Publishers, Inc.

Library of Congress Cataloging-in-Publication Data

Llimós Plomer, Anna.
  [Reciclaje. English]
  Easy earth-friendly crafts in 5 steps / Anna Llimós.
    p. cm. — (Easy crafts in 5 steps)
  Summary: "Presents earth-friendly craft projects that can be made in 5 steps"—Provided by publisher.
  Includes bibliographical references and index.
  ISBN-13: 978-0-7660-3086-2
  ISBN-10: 0-7660-3086-5
  1. Handicraft—Juvenile literature. 2. Recycling (Waste, etc.)—Juvenile literature. I. Title.
  TT160.L5813 2007
  745.5—dc22
                    2007002432

Originally published in Spanish under the title Reciclaje.
Copyright © 2005 PARRAMÓN EDICIONES, S.A., - World Rights.
Published by Parramón Ediciones, S.A., Barcelona, Spain.
Text and development of the exercises: Anna Llimós
Photographs: Nos & Soto

Printed in Spain

10 9 8 7 6 5 4 3 2 1

To Our Readers: We have done our best to make sure all Internet Addresses in this book were active and appropriate when we went to press. However, the author and the publishers have no control over and assume no liability for the material available on those Internet sites or on other Web sites they may link to. Any comments or suggestions can be sent by e-mail to comments@enslow.com or to the address on the back cover.

Every effort has been made to locate all copyright holders of material used in this book. If any errors or omissions have occurred, corrections will be made in future editions of this book.

Contents

 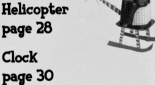

King

MATERIALS

Small plastic container
Cork
Red cord
Bottle cap
Cloth scrap
Different colors of paint
Paintbrush
White glue
Scissors

1 Cut a rectangle out of a cloth scrap. Glue it to the plastic container.

2 Paint the king's face on a cork.

3 Glue the cork on top of the scrap of cloth.

4

4 For the beard and hair, unravel the red cord.

5 Glue the beard and hair on the head. Glue a bottle cap on top for the crown. Let dry.

5

Piggy

MATERIALS

Toilet paper tube
Egg carton
Four corks
Different colors of paint
Paintbrush
White glue
Scissors

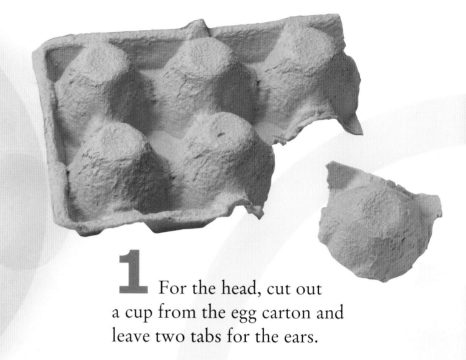

1 For the head, cut out a cup from the egg carton and leave two tabs for the ears.

2 Glue the head to the toilet paper tube.

3 For the legs, glue the corks to the tube. Glue on a cardboard strip from the egg carton for the tail.

4 Paint everything. Let dry.

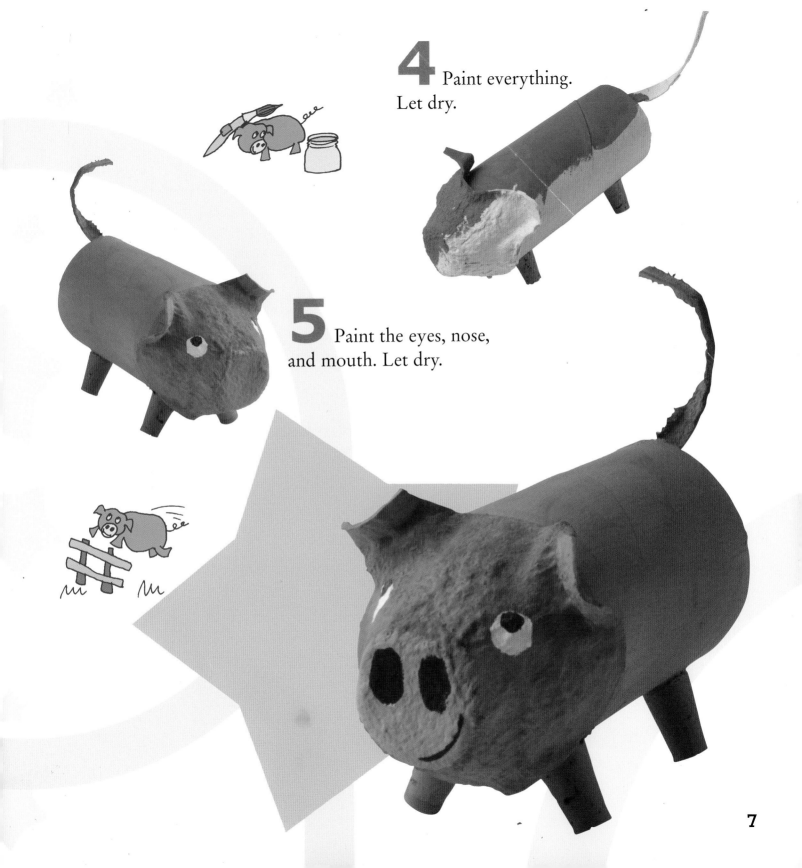

5 Paint the eyes, nose, and mouth. Let dry.

Coin Purse

MATERIALS

Cardboard juice container
Hook and loop fastener
Stapler
Scissors
White glue

1 Flatten the cardboard juice container with the help of an adult.

2 Cut off the top and bottom of the container, leaving a small tab on the top.

3 Fold in the sides of the cardboard container.

4 Fold it in half and staple it in the middle. The coin purse is almost ready.

5 To close the coin purse, glue a strip of hook and loop fastener to the tab and another one opposite it.

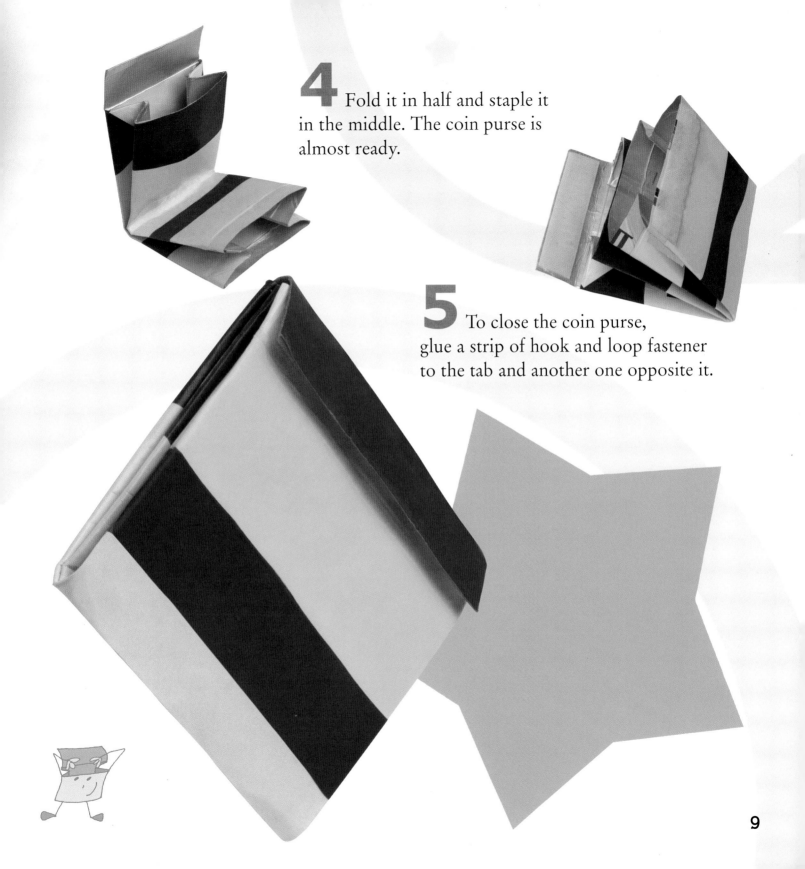

Camel

MATERIALS

Egg carton
Cork
Four clothespins
Different colors of paint
Paintbrush
White glue
Scissors

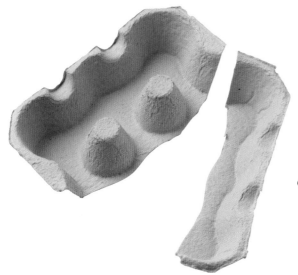

1 For the camel's humps, cut two cups out of the egg carton.

2 Put two clothespins on each hump. They will be the four legs.

3 For the neck, cut out the middle part of an egg carton cup. Glue it to the humps.

10

4 For the head, cut two ears out of the egg carton and glue them to the cork. Glue the cork to the neck.

5 Paint the camel any color you wish. Paint the eyes, nose, and mouth. Let dry.

11

Worm

MATERIALS

Three toilet paper tubes
Two bottle caps
Cork
Different colors of paint
Paintbrush
Stapler
White glue
Scissors

1 Cut the three toilet paper tubes in half the long way.

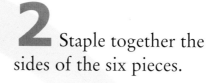

2 Staple together the sides of the six pieces.

3 Paint the pieces any way you wish. You can even paint on stripes!

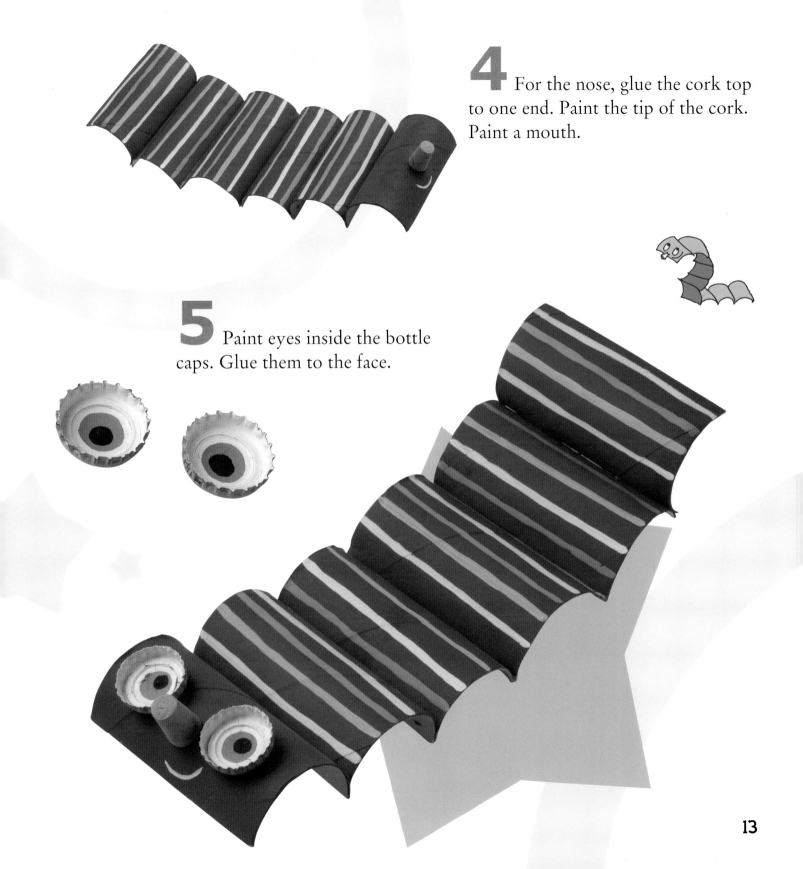

4 For the nose, glue the cork top to one end. Paint the tip of the cork. Paint a mouth.

5 Paint eyes inside the bottle caps. Glue them to the face.

Ladybug

MATERIALS

Egg carton
Small cork
Different colors of paint
Paintbrush
White glue
Scissors

1 Cut two cups out of the egg carton. Cut out part of one of them to make the wings.

2 Paint the wings red and the body black. Let dry.

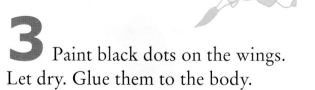

3 Paint black dots on the wings. Let dry. Glue them to the body.

4 Paint a face on the wide part of the cork and glue it to the body.

5 For the antennas, cut out a long strip from the egg carton and paint it black. Glue it to the head. Let dry.

15

Doll

MATERIALS

Two different plastic containers
Two big corks
Cardboard
Magazine page
Thick string
Thin string
Different colors of paint
Paintbrush
Clear tape
White glue
Scissors

1 Ask an adult to help you make a hole in the bottom of each container. Connect them with the thin string. Tie a knot at the end of the string.

2 Cut out two circles of cardboard and paint a face on one of them. Glue them to the string just above the container.

3 Cut hands out of cardboard. Tie a piece of red string around the neck and glue the hands to the ends of the string.

4 For the legs, make a small hole in each cork. Glue a piece of string in the hole of each cork. Attach the string to the inside of the container with clear tape.

5 For the hair, cut out a small rectangle from a magazine page. Make small cuts in the rectangle to make hair.Glue it onto the head.

Hippopotamus

MATERIALS

Mold for storing bottles or wide cardboard tube
Toilet paper tube
Different colors of paint
Paintbrush
Scissors
White glue

1 Cut out one of the bottle cartons and cut off the neck.

2 Use the bottleneck to make four legs, ears, and a tail. Glue them to the body.

3 Paint the hippopotamus. Let dry.

4 Paint the eyes, the nose, and the inside of the ears.

5 Make a bird out of a piece of cardboard, paint it, and glue it onto the hippopotamus.

19

Spinning Top

MATERIALS

Old CD (Ask permission first!)
Different colors of paint
Paintbrush
Toothpick
Cork
Double-sided tape

1 Paint the center of the CD.

2 Paint triangles from the edge to the center of the CD.

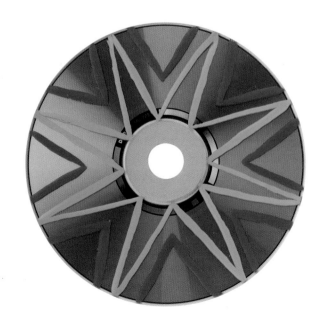

3 Finish painting it with different color triangles.

4 Stick a toothpick in the cork top and paint the cork.

5 Tape the cork onto the CD with double-sided tape.

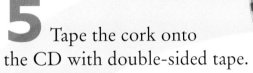

Firefighter

MATERIALS

Empty plastic bottle
Egg carton
Rope
Balloon
Crepe paper
Tissue paper
Red tape
Paint
Modeling clay
Paintbrush
Masking tape
White glue

1 Cover the bottle with red and orange tissue paper. Wrap red tape around the bottle.

2 Make the eyes and the nose out of modeling clay. Glue them onto the bottle cap.

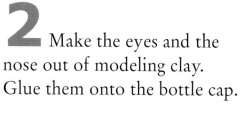

3 Cut out a long strip from a piece of balloon. Tie it around the bottleneck for the arms.

4 Cut out a cup from the egg carton. Paint it, and put it on top of the bottle cap.

5 For the hose, attach some crepe paper to the end of the rope with masking tape and wrap it around the firefighter's body.

23

Box Cake

MATERIALS

Round cardboard box
Paper plate
Plastic container
Plastic cap
Different colors of paint
Paintbrush
Old toothbrush
White glue

1 Paint the box and the plate.

2 Paint stripes around the plate. Use the old toothbrush to sprinkle on some paint.

3 Decorate the side of the box with triangles and dots. Sprinkle on some paint with the toothbrush.

24

4 Paint stripes on the plastic container. Paint its rim red.

5 Glue all the parts one on top of the other. Glue the plastic cap on top as if it were a cherry.

Penguin

MATERIALS

Paper towel tube
Cardboard
Different colors of paint
Paintbrush
Marker
White glue
Stapler
Scissors

1 Draw the shape of a head with a marker on the top of the tube. Cut out around the head.

2 Make the wings and beak out of the left over pieces of tube. Staple the wings to the body and glue the beak on the face.

3 Trace the outline of the tube, and add feet, on a piece of cardboard. Cut it out. Glue it to the bottom of the tube.

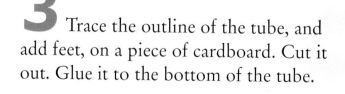

4 Paint the penguin, leaving the stomach and face unpainted.

5 Paint the penguin's beak and feet with orange paint.

Helicopter

MATERIALS

Plastic container
Cardboard
Two toothpicks
Two craft sticks
Cork
Cloth scrap
Different colors of paint
Paintbrush
White glue
Clear tape
Scissors

1 For the window cut out a piece of cloth and glue it to the container.

2 For the landing skids, cut out three pieces of cardboard for each one, and glue them together. Paint stripes on them.

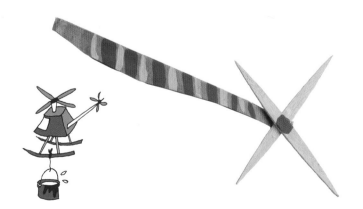

3 For the tail, cut out a strip of cardboard. Glue two toothpicks to the end in the shape of an "X." Paint the tail.

28

4 Attach the landing skids and the tail to the container. Use clear tape for the landing skids. Make a small slot in the container for the tail.

5 For the rotors, glue two craft sticks in the shape of an "X" on top of the cork. Paint them. Glue them to the helicopter.

Clock

MATERIALS

Paper plate
Cork
Paper fastener
Plastic bag
Different colors of paint
Paintbrush
Old toothbrush
Clear tape
Scissors

1 Paint the paper plate.

2 Using a toothbrush, sprinkle different colors of paint. Then, paint the twelve numbers with different colors of paint.

3 To make the clock hands, cut two arrows out of cardboard, one longer than the other. Decorate them with stripes. Make a hole at the end of the clock hands.

4 Fasten the hands to the center of the clock by making a hole with the paper fastener. Glue the cork to the paper fastener.

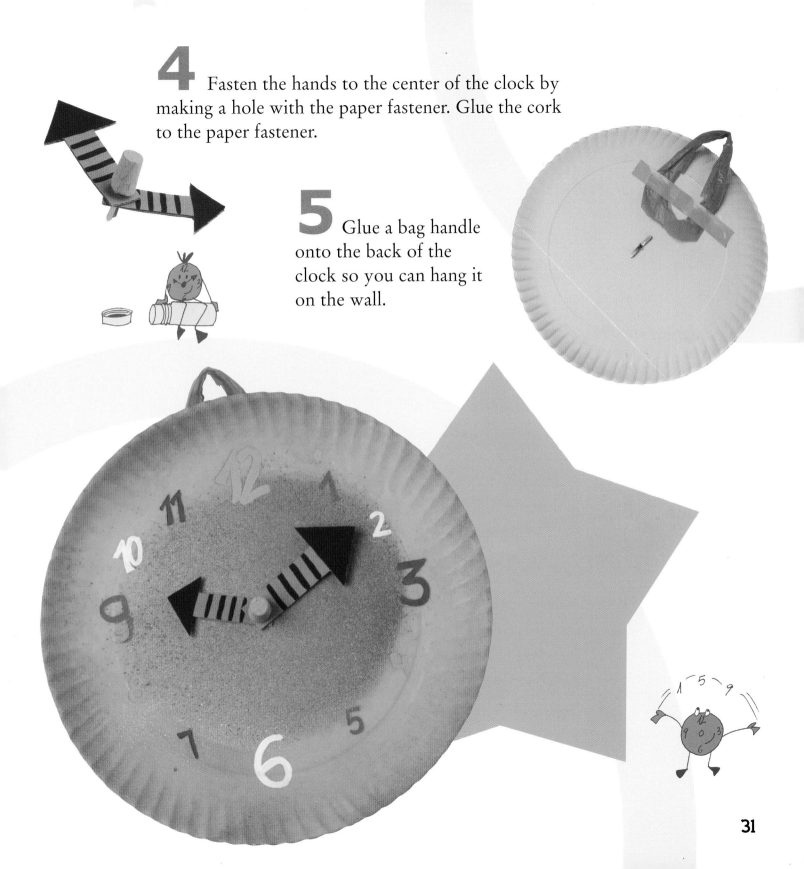

5 Glue a bag handle onto the back of the clock so you can hang it on the wall.

Read About

Books

Lamérand, Violaine. *Crafts from Junk*. Mankato, Minn.: Bridgestone Books, 2003.

Smith, Heather. *Earth Friendly Crafts for Kids: 50 Awesome Things to Make with Recycled Stuff*. New York: Lark Books, 2002.

Sootier, Gillian. *Odds 'n' Ends Art*. Milwaukee, Wis.: Gareth Stevens Pub., 2002.

Internet Addresses

Crafts for Kids at Enchanted Learning
<http://www.enchantedlearning.com/crafts/>

Kids Craft Weekly
<http://www.kidscraftweekly.com/>

Index
Easy to Hard

WITHDRAWN